I Want to Be a TRILLIONAIRE When I Grow Up

Guide Book

WRITTEN BY NEENA RANI SPEER, ESQ.

Using Technology to Breed Success With Lessons in Financial Literacy

I DECLARE I WILL MAKE TRILLIONS

THIS IS MY BOOK, AND I WILL TREAT IT WITH CARE

My Name is:_____

In this book, I will dedicate myself to learning more, trying to answer the questions I don't know, and pushing myself to think outside the box. I know each lesson day I will face 4 questions that will make me a smarter and more financially savvy student, and when I get to the end I will have learned how to

(1) Budget Money, (2) Save Money, and (3) Managing Money using mathematical principles and problem solving.

All Rights Reserved. No part of this publication may be reproduced in any form or by any means, including scanning, photocopying, or otherwise without the publisher's prior written permission.

Disclaimer and Terms of Use: The Author and Publisher have strived to be as accurate and complete as possible in the creation of this book, notwithstanding the fact that they do not warrant or represent at any time that the contents within are accurate due to the rapidly changing nature of the internet. While all attempts have been made to verify information provided in this publication, the Author and the publisher assume no responsibility for errors, omissions, or contrary interpretation of the subject matter herein. Any perceived slights of specific persons, peoples, or organizations are unintentional. In practical advice books, like anything else in life, there are no guarantees of income made. Readers are cautioned to rely on their judgment about their circumstances to act accordingly. This book is not intended for use as a legal, business, accounting, or financial advice source. All readers are advised to seek the services of competent professionals in the legal, business, accounting, and finance fields. This is for informational use only. Not legal advice. An attorney-client relationship is not formed by viewing and receiving information attached to The Neena R. Speer Law Firm LLC's social media pages @neenarspeerlawfirm. "No representation is made that the quality of the legal services to be performed is greater than the quality of legal services performed by other lawyers."

For information on quantity sales: Special discounts are available on quantity purchases for corporations, associations, U.S. trade bookstores, wholesalers, and independent booksellers

Copyright © 2022 Neena the LAST Brand LLC
All Rights Reserved.
ISBN: 978-1-7366939
ISBN-13: 978-1-7366939-5-7

"Dedication

Donnie Ray Speer (my late father) for all the dedication and discipline you inspired in me.

Acknowledgments

I want to take the time to acknowledge all the people that I felt led to me creating this book, and I want to recognize the person who who always pushed discipline throughout my childhood, and that is my late father, Donnie Ray Speer (my poppa bear). Donnie Ray Speer is a man to who I can't quite use all of the English language words to do justice, but he cared about his family. He loved harder than any person I've ever met. He gave so much to the world. One thing I loved about Donnie Ray Speer is that he was present for every single moment of our lives. This mainly happened after he began having health issues with his legs and overall. However, before that, he was the only person making model dioramas and pirate flags so that I didn't have to go to school ashamed of my assignments. I know when people think of dads, they see an intimidating figure that will put the fear of God in any man trying to trick his daughter or the world. They imagine that he towers over people. Though he was 6'8", my dad was the kindest, most loving man to my sister, my mom, and myself that I have ever known. He loved people, and he never missed an opportunity to make you feel loved when you needed it most. That is the most challenging part of the business because my dad had passed away when I finally hit my stride in my business. I wanted nothing more than to share every single moment with him when I finally adhered to the lessons he had always been planting in my sister and me completely. He did get to see me pass the bar, which is phenomenal because I started to find my road to success towards the end of 2019. I had no idea I would lose him at that moment. That awakened something in me to keep going, and my sister and my mom were the main people I wanted to cherish every moment with from that day forward. So, he brought us all back together with a common cause to keep fighting.

I want to acknowledge my mom for giving me a space to chase every single fantasy that I had in this business journey with financial peace. My mom, Rajesh Speer, has made more sacrifices to ensure that she could support us as we chased financial freedom as she has already achieved. My mom listens when I'm broken, picks me up, and tells me there is better coming. Mama is the only person that I would pitch any business idea before taking action. If my momma can understand it, so can you. I have cherished the pandemic in some respects because I have never observed more movie nights than we ever did before. Most times, we even try to set a rule where we just don't work. Well, at least not entirely, and we just relax in front of the TV.

I want to acknowledge my sister, Smita Speer because she is the one who always believes in me and is the first to buy everything in my retail store to support me. She takes the time to listen to me and hear me when I face insecurities in myself. She is also my most honest and thoughtful critic. She can deliver the blows of reality I need so I don't take myself so seriously and keep me from seeing bad things in people who are not there. She is the person who is genuinely her renaissance woman and can do things I cannot imagine by just applying what she finds in a tutorial or course. Smita has been the one to edit my manuscripts, papers and just tell me that "it's all gonna be OK" on my worst days. Smita is my guiding light and the person who holds me accountable when I don't want to be held accountable. I spent a lot of time cultivating and perfecting my relationship with Smita (my sis) and my mom to be a better daughter, better sister, and better person. I don't always get it right. However, they still push me and love me enough to tell me to "fix my face and my attitude" so that I can keep going. These are the family support team that pushed and still pushes me every single moment and supported me when I was broken. Many people couldn't see me suffering, but those three above always knew when I needed the help most, and when I finally was able to find joy, they were too. That is powerful.

I would also like to acknowledge my best friend Tsipporah (Tt), who, shortly after my junior year in college, I don't think I would have had the confidence to author this book had it not been for your undying support throughout this process. I can tell you one thing for sure Tt was my first friend who came with a bonus family, and her mom Daphne Christopher gives me more support on social media than I ever thought possible. I have never met a family that's more supportive of the little things that I and their "real children" embark on. I met Tt when I didn't have a lot of faith in people in undergraduate. Tt has supported me throughout my undergraduate career, law school, post-law school, and lawyer and non-profit endeavors. Everybody needs a Tt in their lives to help them when times get rough.

I would also like to acknowledge my other friend Lauren Summers for her friendship as I grew at Howard University and even more after that fateful day at the diner. That was the day that led to a friendship that went far deeper than just going to undergraduate together. You were there to support me throughout my law school process, and you kept supporting me even when med school was on the horizon. Sometimes in life, we need somebody who will make sure that we are always prioritizing our mental health, our wellness and mental safety, and our emotional security. That person for me is you, Lauren.

I would also like to acknowledge my other friend Alayna Smith-McFee for everything she does to support and care for me. Friends in life never give up on you, even when you want to give up on yourself. Your baby Phillip junior brings me nothing but life, and just getting to see you graduate with him while eating his snacks in the audience, just how you planned it last year, was the biggest blessing ever. Your "Grandma B" is forever memorialized in this book as one of the few people there I saw pouring into you from day one. Though you didn't always have the support you needed from everyone in your life, she always made you feel like you had a safe place to land. You deserve that and more, and I am so honored that I get to experience even a fraction of that love as your friend.

I would also like to take the time to acknowledge my mentors and my mentees over the years. Though sometimes we do fall out of touch because of life over it was the end of our season together, I appreciate you so much for what positive uplift and encouragement you have given to me. I have tons of mentees, so I cannot name them all. However, there is one that I want to mention because this young little girl kept me from dropping out of law school. Her name is key Kedriona Tubbs, and she was the first person I had to keep a promise to for mentorship. I swore to her that I was a mentor for life for her. I promised that I was not just there as a community service line on my resume. That was a promise that was extremely hard to keep at first because after the spring semester of my first year of law school; her school lost track of her. the mentoring program that I was volunteering for also lost track of her. They even tried to put me with a new mentee. Still, this did not work for me because I simply could not break my promise. This little girl makes me a better mentor and person each day. The day that I found her again was one of the happiest moments I have ever had throughout my long journey.

I Want To Be a Trillionaire When I Grow Up

Modules for Success

Financial Literacy Consultant

This book is a must-have study guide and workbook for students looking to broaden or master their skills of understanding money scenarios. It is perfect for anyone who wishes to enter the real-world and is an excellent complementary tool to prepare for the road ahead

With this book, you will be able to:

Define key money terms as it related to real-life examples

Learn the strategies to apply math principles to an ideal job plan

Test your knowledge with technological tests

Once a week, we are graced with the presence of Attorney Neena, and she does an amazing job with financial literacy with our students. She always makes the lessons engaging and fun. We've done activities where they've picked careers, made a budget, saved, and of course big prizes at the end. We appreciate Ms. Neena's enthusiasm that she brings each and every time to such an important concept for all of our students.

Maria
Fairfield High Preparatory School

About The Author

Neena Speer, Esq.

Neena Speer graduated from the University of Alabama School of Law in 2017, and she attended her undergraduate studies at Howard University in from 2010-2014. She is Principal of her book, speaking, and consulting company, an executive director of her own non-profit, an award winning trademark law firm owner, and a Two Time Amazon Best Seller for her books, Dear Future Lawyer and Dear Future CEO®ANI.

LET'S GO ON AN ADVENTURE
NENE IS A TRILLIONAIRE, BUT HOW?

01: Values + Money
The Story of Shanté and Leyoncé — 09

02: Social Media + Money
The Story of Kira — 12

03: Jobs + Money
The Story of The Job Game — 16

04: Intro to Biz + Money
The Story of Kira and Shanté — 20

05: Trademarks + Money
The Story of Danc.itivity — 25

06: Copyrights + Money
The Story of Marco vs. Leyoncé — 29

07: Patents + Money
The Story of Sketch and Pike — 34

08: Education + Money
The Story of Penelope and Roger — 39

09: Struggle + Money
The Story of Mud Jones — 44

10: Debt and Money
The Story of Stacy's Bad Credit — 49

11: Investing + Money
The Story of Penelope the Event Planner — 54

12: Planning + Money
The Story of Penelope the Event Planner — 59

RESOURCES — 66
NeNe Says Do This
10 Tips To Save Your Business Money
How to Create Your Own for a GIPHY Channel and Apply for GIFS
5 Reasons You Need an LLC For Your New Business
Virtual Games List

MEET NENE TRILLIONAIRE
The Real Truth of NeNe Trillionaire — 71

LESSON
01: Values + Money

I Want To Be a Trillionaire When I Grow Up

The Story of Shanté and Leyocé

Shanté always admired Leyoncé. As children, Shanté saw Leyoncé spend money on luxury items like gowns and toys. Shanté always **struggled with money** growing up and Leyoncé **spent money on everything.** One day, they met NeNe, and she introduced them to a way to look at money in a way that made Leyoncé and Shanté both see where they could improve on money management skills.

She told them about **a budget.** NeNe told Shanté that she could have the nice gowns and toys like Leyoncé had, but she may have to find them at different places. Shanté did not believe her at first, but NeNe showed her **the same dress at the local thrift store** that was much more affordable and helped her discover on eBay that the expensive toy was listed for way less. Shanté also showed Leyoncé the same thing, but Leyoncé just wanted a shopping friend to spend time with even though it was exciting to save money.

After NeNe came to town, Shanté and Leyoncé who bonded over budgets started going thrifting together and realized they were happiest spending time window shopping together instead of spending money. They produced a big idea to run a babysitting service in the summers so that they could buy more cool gowns of course but they also wanted to get their first cell phone so they could call each other every day.

01. What do you think a budget is?

02. Why did Shanté like budgeting?

03. Why did Leyoncé like budgeting?

04. What made both Leyoncé and Shanté the happiest?

What You Will Learn Today:

The lessons throughout this section are for those who have struggled with money and who also tend to spend more quickly. It is all about reflecting on what you value in terms of wants, needs, and luxury through the lens of money. The way in which you grew up matters, and it is important to know what budgeting looks like. Together, we will learn how to budget. This section is about how knowing your values can guide how one spends money.

What You Will Learn Today:

- Growing Up **with Money Everywhere**: does not mean you understand how to manage or budget well
- Growing Up **with Money Struggles**: does not mean you cannot have nice things or afford them
- Growing Up **with a Budget**: does not mean that you will never overspend or never fall on hard times

Values to Learn:

Although one can have many money stories, how will you be remembered?

- The Value of Friendship is more valuable than money
- Working with your friends can lead to meeting your financial goals faster
- Being creative with ways to earn money include side hustles
- You can lose money quickly when your values do not have a pure purpose
- **Allen Iverson (famous NBA player)** lost all his money quickly... do you know why?
- You are not limited to just one job
- How you see yourself is how you will be (ex. If you see yourself as broke, you will be that way) – **Change your thoughts, change your life**

Money Hustles for You:

- Blogging
- Secret shopping
- Surveys
- Anchor.Fm (Podcasting App)
- McCormick's Tester
- Carvertise

Draw What You Learned:

LESSON
02: Social Media + Money

The Story of Kira

Kira spent most of her time learning the new dances on TikTok. One day, she created her own dance. She went on her phone and posted her dance moves with DC Cred on her page before she went to sleep. Her dance was so popular that by morning it was all she could see on her timeline. So, she decided to launch a dance class via her social media, but she had no idea how to market it. One day, she met NeNe, and she introduced her to the money tools on all social media such as lead magnets.

Kira was so confused about lead magnets, and she asked NeNe to explain. NeNe showed Kira that if she created a tutorial video of creating your own dance and gave access to that video to people who gave her their emails, she would have a community of support. NeNe showed her how to take that community of support and make them join a Facebook group that she pours into.

Kira is blown away that she can use social media to do something so simple. Kira also discovered she had 1000 followers on TikTok which meant she could go LIVE and earn money by teaching more dances.

01. What do you think a lead magnet is?

02. Why did Kira like using social media?

03. What is a tutorial video?

04. What made Kira the happiest?

What You Will Learn Today:

The lessons throughout this section are for those who have struggled with understanding the importance of social media to learn, network, and leverage your brand. It is all about reflecting on some of the most popular platforms are **TikTok, Clubhouse, Instagram, Facebook, LinkedIn, and YouTube.** The lesson goes on into a few creative ways that one can use social media like adding payment processors, **Linktrees, and providing valuable content.** One important note from this lesson is to not rely solely on social media. Together, we will learn how to sell services and goods for a business and the idea behind marketing early for kids for brand deals. This section is about how knowing your social media is not just a time waster but can be the ULTIMATE BUSINESS TOOL.

A Note To Keep In Mind:

- **Social Media Influencers**: this can be the easiest career to create for yourself if you study it
- **Making Your Own Spaces**: you can use WORDPRESS to make a free website today and start telling your story
- **Put the Phone Down**: just because you plugged in for "work" doesn't mean it is all that you do, work on yourself and how you want to be known

Values to Learn:

Although one can have many apps, how will you be remembered?

- The Value of Community can be more valuable than money
- Using your creativity and gifts can lead to meeting your financial goals faster
- Being creative with ways to earn money include social media strategies
- Social Media is not always safe for you
- **Supa Cent (famous makeup artist)** made $1,000,000 in 90 Minutes... do you know why?
- You are not limited to just one platform
- Social media is important for social networking and leveraging your brand
- Telling your story on social media can be scary and hard, but it is better if done strategically (ex. If you want to be an astronaut, then consider using your social media to share tips on how to prepare for a career as an astronaut and telling your story to apply) – **Change your focus, change your life**

Money Hustles for You:

- Brand Deals
- Podcast on Facebook
- Subscriptions on IG
- Brand Marketplace TikTok
- Pinned Link on Clubhouse
- Lnk.bio account
- Podia for selling courses
- Facebook Groups for Paid Groups
- Zoom for Webinars
- Email Marketing with Mailchimp
- Bookings/Appointments with Calendly

Draw What You Learned:

LESSON
03: Jobs + Money

The Story of The Job Game

NeNe met up with Leyoncé to teach her an amazing game that she could play to pick a dream job for herself. She told her to decide how much she wanted to get paid per year first, which was known as **her annual salary.** After she decided her desired salary, NeNe gave her a task to **divide that number by the number of days a year she wanted to work, this is known as the 219 working days daily formula.**

The hardest part was next because after she learned that her **dream salary would require her to make $4,570 per day.** To earn $1,000,000 seems hard, but imagine if you worked less days and earned money that met your **daily sales goal** with one sale? Leyoncé was so intrigued because she learned how to budget the last time, she talked to NeNe. So, she asked what's next.

NeNe told her to **make a list of thirty things she could do to make $4,570 per day.** This was a list of all her skills and talents known using an activity called mind storming. Leyoncé was overwhelmed. There was no way she could think of thirty things, but she tried anyway. When she finally listed all of her options, she had a few different career options: **chef, writer, or an inventor of Black girl deodorant.** NeNe was so impressed by her creativity, and this new job game was something Leyoncé was so excited to tell her friend Shanté all about.

01. What do you think a salary is?

02. How do decide how much money you want to make per year?

03. What did Leyoncé produce in her mind storm that was creative?

04. How much do you need to make per day to make a million dollars in a year?

What You Will Learn Today:

The lessons throughout this section are for what you must know about what it takes to get your dream job, the importance of networking within your communities to learn more about unique jobs, and finding people within the career field you are interested in. It is also important to think about the average salary if you want to be an entrepreneur, an employee, or both. If you know the job you want, all you have to do is research what the average salary is for it, find the top 3 people in that job on Google and ask them if you can shadow them. If you repeat that step over and over again, eventually you will find a mentor in the field.

A Note To Keep In Mind:

- **You Don't Have to Pick Just One Job**: many adults try to tell you to pick one job, but I say dream in threes and fours and whatever you feel like you can do. **Just make sure you can be proud of yourself!**
- **Let your day job fund your dream**: it's okay to get a job that helps you reach your goals, and in the off time, you can plan your exit plan
- **You can create your own job**: being your own boss is truly possible, but if you lack discipline and cannot get tasks done or follow simple rules for yourself, you will find a lot of hard days before it gets easier

Values to Learn:

Although one can have many jobs, how will you be remembered?

- The Value of Believing in Your Talents can be more valuable than money
- Using your talents to create your own job or invent something new can lead to meeting your financial goals faster
- Being creative with ways to earn money include having several job options
- Having a job doesn't have to be a 9am-5pm, BUT THE PANDEMIC showed us that companies will let you **work from home** so try to figure out a combo option
- KFC (what's the story behind the secret recipe) how did he protect, who produced it, and when did he start his company?
- You are not limited to just one job
- Do you know if you want to be an **entrepreneur** (someone who creates something new), an **employee** (someone who works for a company) or **BOTH?**
- Finding a job is scary, but those who prepare will be ready when an opportunity opens up (ex. Volunteer, create a **resume**, keep track of your progress, and ask for reviews and feedback) – **Demand the job you want for yourself, not the one someone else chose**

Money Hustles for You:

- Teach Courses/Virtual or In-Person
- Paid Speaker
- Write Books
- Launch a Podcast
- Create a unique digital product
- Become a virtual assistant
- Be a social media manager

Draw What You Learned:

LESSON
04: Intro to Biz + Money

I Want To Be a Trillionaire When I Grow Up

The Story of Kira and Shanté

Kira started her TikTok dance Facebook club, and she is excited to meet one of her students and then she got an email from Facebook inviting her to join their bonuses program. In less than two months she had made so many 1 min videos and she released a new one every day, but she added inspirational messages to the videos. People on Facebook went crazy about the REELS! At this point, Kira had a Facebook group (subscribers), a reel released every day (a digital marketing strategy), and now an influencer status (with payouts happening every time five videos hit more than 100 views on Reels), but she had no idea how to turn any of that into a business.

People were paying her money, but she wanted to understand business structure and rules. One day, Kira meets one of her dance students IRL and it just happens to be Shanté. Now, Shanté was so excited to meet her teacher that she had nothing but questions. Shanté knew NeNe had helped her learn some pretty hard words. So, she called her when Kira looked confused with the questions.

The first question NeNe answered was about business structure. She told Kira that every business needs a business name. Kira thought long and hard about what she would name her business, but NeNe stopped her to tell her a business trick about how names are best created when you make up new words and new ways to define your brand. So, she tried an exercise with her, what do you want people to feel when they think of your business? Kira's answer was "well, I want them to love their unique bodies and dance moves enough to make their own." NeNe smiled and said, "that is what you will tell them in your business name."

After a tough brainstorm, Kira yelled out, "I got it! What about Danc.itivity like Dance and Positivity mashed into one word? Now, NeNe smiled again and said, "That name is so amazing." So, the next step was to pick her business shape "her Pokémon for her business type." Let's be honest NeNe knew there were many business shapes, but the one she recommended for Kira was the one she hopes would be easiest to start. It was an LLC which means a Limited Liability Company.

With this business type on the game board, Kira was almost ready to start her business. She was just missing one more thing...the rules to play. This part NeNe compared to learning the rules of a sports. There were things that only your players can do, but you are the coach and even if there are rules you don't know, you are responsible for leading your team to victory.

"The best way to create good business rules is to study good business owners. The one I always like to think of is the 11 year old who invented a popsicle," said NeNe. This time Kira smiled and Shanté caught on quickly and decided to study the kid who invented the popsicle. NeNe was sure that Shanté and Kira had a good understanding of basic business rules now, so she told them to start planning their business and report back before playing the game!

01. What did Kira decide was her business name?

02. What type of business is the easiest to form?

03. How do you create good business rules?

04. What did Kira and Shanté need to do before they reported back to NeNe?

What You Will Learn Today:

The lessons throughout this section are asking you to think about the age of the kid was who invented popsicle and how one must properly set up a business if they want to be successful . It also talks about being a board or a director of a business or owner at a certain age. It goes on to explain the steps you may take to become an inventor which include defining a problem that people have and creating a solution to fix that problem.

But, this section is more about what business owners to do before starting a business. This section shows you that though you may want to work for a company when you grow up, **YOU CAN ALSO WORK FOR YOURSELF!**

A Note To Keep In Mind:

- **Employee:** this is when you work for someone else, and they run the business on the backend [COLLECT PAYCHECKS]
- **Entrepreneur:** this is when you create something new that the market has never seen or improve something that already exists that people will pay you for [CREATES SOMETHING NEW, AND RESPONSIBLE FOR BUSINESS SUCCESS]
- **Being Your Own Boss:** owning a business is an amazing feeling because you decide your hours, but it is also a lot of hard work that you cannot be lazy about [IT COSTS TO BE THE BOSS]

Values to Learn:

Although one can have many businesses, how will you be remembered?

- The Value of 9-5 job can be more valuable than money to funding your dream
- Inventing something new can lead to meeting your financial goals faster
- Being creative with ways to earn money include starting a business or inventing something
- There is no age limit to creating something that is protectable
- **7-Year Old Business Owner (graphic designer** ... do you know her name and how she did it?
- You are not limited to waiting until you grow up from making a money for yourself
- Learning how to math is actually very important in **business budgets**
- You can be talented and earning money, but without strategy you will see it is hard to repeat or measure why you are successful (ex. If you have a b, you will rely on Facebook to work for you to be successful) –BUMP social media, get your own community offline

Money Hustles for You:

- Free Business Phone Number: **Google Voice**
- Free Business Blog and Website: **WordPress**
- Free Business Email: **firstnamelastname@gmail.com Gmail**
- Free Course Platforms: **Podia** (just launched in June 2022)
- Free Virtual Business Cards: **Hi.Hello**
- Free Podcast: **Zoom or Google Meet**
- Free Business Classes: **Small Business Administration (SBA) in your state**
- Free Legal Help: **Law School Clinics, Free Legal and Pro Bono Clinics**
- Free Social Media Top Questions in Your Industry Search Tool: **Answerthepublic.com**
- Building Business Credit from a bank loan or credit card
- Free E-Commerce Site: **SquareUp.Com**

Draw What You Learned:

LESSON

05: Trademarks + Money

The Story of Danc.itivity

Kira was ready to launch her business Danc.itivity , but she ran into Drew who saw her Facebook Dance group and decided to try to beat Kira to protect her domain name and get paid big. Now Kira had been smart and protected all the social media accounts for @Danc.itivity to protect her BUSINESS NAME. Drew knew that she had not protected the website, so he bought danceitivity.com before Kira could. Drew told her he'd sell it back to her for $10,000.

Kira thought long and hard about what to do and remembered Shanté had given her NeNe's number in case she ran into any issues. Kira called NeNe and explained what Drew had done. NeNe smiled and told her to buy the same website but call it danceitivity.co. Drew did not expect that. He quickly called Kira and said that he'd be happy to sell her the .com website for $1,000 instead. However, Kira smiled and said no.

Without telling Drew, she hired NeNe for filing her trademark application. She filed a 1A application which is a stronger application to file, and it took about 15 months to get it protected. By this time, Drew had invested about $250 into owning this domain that he wanted to sell. In the 15th month, NeNe secured Kira's trademark certificate for her. After that, NeNe wrote Drew a letter and said that he would be required to abandon the domain danceitivity.com or face a lawsuit.

She also sent this to the company he bought the domain from, and they deactivated the account right away. Drew wasted $250.00 on a domain he can no longer hold, and he cannot get that back, but Kira put in the intense work it required to get her brand ready for a trademark application. That year, she secured a TV show called Danc.itivity® with Kira.

If it had not been for Drew, Kira would never have known about the not so nice part of business. People are always trying to make money, but they didn't learn about having good values when trying to reach that goal. Kira also learned that when you start a business, creating a unique name is actually a business success strategy.

01. What do you think a trademark is?

02. Why did Drew try to steal Kira's website domain?

03. Why did Kira call NeNe?

04. What did NeNe do to help Kira beat Drew?

What You Will Learn Today:

The lessons throughout this section are for those who have struggled with understanding the reasons why businesses owners get tricked in business. It also shows how to beat someone known as a **domain squatter** with outsmarting them, and It talks about the stronger trademark application to file if you have been in business for a while. It also shows you how having to go through the awfully long process of trademarks, creating a unique name, and doing an extensive search can make you level up your business to put it on a national scale.

A Note To Keep In Mind:

Strength of the Name Activity

- **Fanciful -** Strongest- made up word/symbol/phrase
- **Arbitrary -** Stronger – word/symbol/phrase given new meaning
- **Suggestive -** Weak but still strong – word/symbol/phrase has traits in common with service/good
- **Descriptive -** Weaker – word/symbol/phrase describes exactly what is being sold
- **Generic -** Weakest – word/symbol/phrase is the same what is being sold

Values to Learn:

Although one can have many words/symbols/phrases, how will you be remembered?

- The Value of a Brand's Trademark can be more valuable than money
- Using your resources and advisers in a smart way can lead to meeting your financial goals faster
- Being creative with ways to earn money include filing to own the trademark or domain squatting
- Every person who sees your success won't congratulate
- **Black Girl Magic (was stolen from the original phrase creator)** because of what reason… do you know why?
- **Lady A (had to sue for the right to use her name)** because of what reason… do you know why?
- **Just because someone owns a trademark doesn't mean they can block your freedom of expression** Think Barbie Girl case
- Paying a professional to fight your battles for you is important to build a strong brand
- Protecting your brand is important, but it is better if done strategically (ex. If you encounter a problem, hire a pro and work extremely hard on improving your business to overcome any person trying to steal your brand) –**They can't outwork you.**

Money Trademark Hustles for You:

- Protect Your TikTok Username
- Protect Your Business Name
- Protect Your Logo
- Protect Your Social Media Series Title
- Protect Your Web Domain
- Protect Your Personal Name
- Protect Your Catchphrases
- Protect Your Smells Protect Your Sounds
- Protect Your Colors
- Protect Your Podcast Titles
- Protect Your Book Series
- Protect Your Signature Event Name

Draw What You Learned:

LESSON
06: Copyrights + Money

The Story of Marco vs. Leyoncé

Marco was a skilled photographer, and he also captured amazing videos of his friends. He also used to take pictures of famous celebrities. Leyoncé was so excited to do her photoshoot in her new outfit with Marco.

Now, Marco was new to business, so he charged $250 for his hour-long photo shoot with Leyoncé. She took 400 pics in that time slot. Now, when she and Marco had finished, she wanted all 400 photos.

Marco told her that that was impossible and told her to pick her favorite 20 photos. Leyoncé was upset because they were her photos and she wanted them, so she asked Marco for a refund. Marco said no because he had done the work and sent her the best 20 photos in her set. Leyoncé never used any of them because of the disagreement. Marco was upset, but he knew that he met a girl named NeNe when he started out who told

him that "whoever creates it, owns it." So, he decided to create an artistic piece with the photos he had taken to tell an amazing story.

The local art gallery saw his photos one day and wanted to have him host an exhibit with the photos he'd taken of Leyoncé. So, in just 3 weeks, he was paid thousands of dollars for his photos. Leyoncé found out that he was making money off her image, and she was angry. Those pictures were hers, or so she thought. She called NeNe crying about what had happened. NeNe nodded as Leyoncé told her what was troubling her. This time, however, NeNe didn't have a solution that Leyoncé liked. She told her about the rule that Marco used was right.

She told Leyoncé about why it is important for her photographers to sign clear contracts for photography that grant her something called the exclusive copyright rights. NeNe always had a hack though. She said, go somewhere new, get your makeup done, and bring a tripod. You can capture the most amazing photos on your own. Then, those photos will be fully yours.

So, she found an HBCU Homecoming and started capturing content. Leyoncé's one photo was on an HBCU Homecoming Yardfest and that one photo went viral on the internet. Her photo had everyone captivated and it indeed broke the internet. Everyone kept resharing it and demanded she get a modeling contract. Within a month, a modeling agency called Leyoncé and asked her if she wanted to collaborate with them. Marco didn't have those pictures, and Leyoncé owned the full rights to them. The modeling contract was for $50,000 which was more than Marco made on her old photos.

01.   What do you think exclusive copyright rights is?

02.   Why did Leyoncé get upset?

03.   Why did Marco get to make money off of Leyoncé's photos?

04.   What made Leyoncé the happiest?

What You Will Learn Today:

The lessons throughout this section are for those who have struggled with understanding the copyright ownership rule that "whoever creates it, owns it." A business owner must properly strategize how to secure and protect content with copyright. An important note is that one may copyright in many forms of creative and unique expression. It lasts the owner's entire lifetime plus many years after. This section asks, you to reflect on whether one must prioritize copyrighting a group of items or one item at a time.

You can also think about how much money one can sue for to protect your brand. It also explains Fair Use Doctrine for those who own a copyright because sometimes people can use your copyright. This doctrine is about as confusing as the proper way to drive in a roundabout with too many turns and circles. The lesson goes on into a few creative ways that one can use copyrights to monetize your brand, business, or everyday creations. One important note from this lesson is to **not rely on copyright alone to protect your brand**.

Together, we will learn how to **write our own books**, talk about the process of protecting ourselves from thieves, book covers, the sales process and why kid's books are fun to create and sell with a plan. This section is about how knowing **YOUR STORY MATTERS** and **YOU ARE NOT JUST A KID**. You can be an author right now with an inventive mind, a creative voice, and **A MOTIVATION TO LEAVE AN IMPACT.**

A Note To Keep In Mind:

- **Fair Use Doctrine:** the easiest way to explain is that if its educational or some other exception, then you are not liable for copying the name, phrase, or creative expression. But what really is "educational fair use"?
- **Copyright Your Photos, Your Videos, Your Podcasts:** nothing is off limits, but remember this if you get help with homework then you didn't really "do if it meets the copyright standard.
- **Put the Phone Down:** just because you plugged in for "work" doesn't mean it is all that you do, work on yourself and how you want to be known

Values to Learn:

Although one can have many phots/videos/original sounds/original dances, how will you be remembered?

- The Value of a Photographer's photo rights can be more underestimated until it is **too late**
- Using your resources and advisers can teach you how to beat someone in business rights
- Being creative with just a cell phone and paying attention to angles, lighting and **being yourself can really break the internet**
- **Having someone create something for you without a contract in place can be bad**
- B. Simone (famous celebrity) made a huge copyright mistake... do you know what it was?
- You are not limited in what you can protect. Think: **books, presentations, website designs, computer code, photos, videos, choreography, merchandise designs, songs, poems, beats and more**

- Clear communication upfront is important to be able to make smart business decisions later
- Being willing to write your idea down is scary, but what's worse is letting someone copy something like your **TikTok dance or your business plan** and make money off of it because you didn't write it down

Money Copyright Hustles for You:

- Stage Names
- Masters + Beats
- Instrumentals
- Lyrics
- Art (paint, sculpt, etc.)
- Digital Proofs
- Signature
- Course Materials
- Sizzle Reels
- Images
- Videos
- Interview Audio
- Podcasts
- E-Books
- Books
- Pitch Decks

Draw What You Learned:

LESSON
07: Patents + Money

The Story of Sketch and Pike

Pike was planning to **patent his sketches of this new breathable sock wear** that kept your feet from stinking. Thanks to a unique weaving design method for the socks, they were more breathable. Sketch took one of the socks that Pike had been working on and went to create his own competing sock design business. Pike saw that Sketch had copied him and went to market his product, but Sketch was so popular, and no one would believe Pike that Sketch had copied him. **Pike lost hope for years until one day Leyoncé his childhood best friend came to visit his sock shop.**

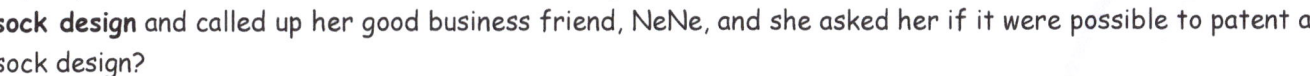

She tried to motivate him, but Pike had given up and couldn't keep up with Sketch's followers who were waiting on the next major thing he'd create. One day Leyoncé discovered **the sketches of the original sock design** and called up her good business friend, NeNe, and she asked her if it were possible to patent a sock design?

NeNe told her that it was possible, but that Pike would need a good marketing team for 15-20 years because after that **anyone could profit off his design.** So, she asked NeNe the steps to secure a patent. First, they had to get a patent lawyer and find out if the sock design was patentable.

After that, they had to **put money aside to pay for the patent process**. From there, if it were approved, he would be able to take action against Sketch for copying his design process. However, it may be a difficult and costly legal battle. Leyoncé decided to be an investor for Pike. She knew that Sketch could only make something new if he copied Pike, and thus she used a small amount of her modeling money and did the modeling marketing for free for his socks and helped him get his design patented with a lawyer.

Many months later, the patent was approved and Leyoncé's investment helped him protect his design. She became a silent **investor in Pike's company**, and he paid her for all of her ads and marketing for future campaigns.

After that, **Pike had his attorney reach out to Sketch with his patent** certificate and told him to cease all uses of his **design immediately.** All of Sketch's businesses and profits were shut down and he was forced to leave the sock business. He came to Pike years later and said, "what you did was the most amazing business power move I've seen in business. I really want to **apologize for trying to make a quick buck on something that was really your creation."**

Can you forgive me?" Pike

smiled and said, "I already forgave you." Pike went on to **teach Sketch how to produce his own unique thing** and realized he was a skilled app designer. So, when Pike was ready to launch his Sock Design Customize Me App, he called Sketch to do it and told him how to file his own patent. They both went on to make millions on their own unique inventions and even though Sketch started off on the wrong foot, he eventually found the right steps to success.

01. What do you think a patent is?

02. Why did Pike want a patent?

03. What did Sketch steal from Pike?

04. What made both Sketch and Pike make up?

What You Will Learn Today:

The lessons throughout this section are for those who have struggled with understanding patents and how long they can last. The lesson goes on into a few items you can patent especially retelling the story of the Popsicle patent. One important note from this lesson is to not fail to protect your design patents early on and make sure you save a ton of money for a good patent lawyer. Together, we will learn how to understand why patents are useful for a business and the idea behind marketing your patent before it expires and then everyone can use it.

This section is about how knowing your patent can bring profit to your business, but you must get a solid legal team and action plan. **There are special kinds of examples, but one thing that most people don't talk about is how much you can make with a patent. The cost of a patent lawyer is also very high, but investors are great sources for help.**

You can also think about how kids can be the creator of their own wealth. Inventions like popsicle sticks and peanut butter were able to change lives. You are truly limitless.

Together, we will learn how to create our own inventions, talk about the process of protecting ourselves from thieves, investors, and our own family. This section is about knowing your IDEAS MATTER and you are not JUST A KID. You can be an INVENTOR right now with an inventive mind, a creative voice, and **A MOTIVATION TO LEAVE AN IMPACT.**

A Note To Keep In Mind:

- **What are things you can invent and protect (a.k.a what can you patent)?** This protects the design or process by which you do something or even the method you use to do something
- **A patent doesn't last as long as you think: 15 Years for Design Patents, 20 Years for Utility Patents**
- Patent secures your designs and way of doing things
- Patents **are expensive**

Values to Learn:

Although one can have many inventions, how will you be remembered?

- The Value of Sincere Apologies and Changed Behavior can solve more problems than money
- Using your creativity and gifts can lead to meaningful ways to help your friends
- Being creative with ways to solve problems can include **a sock design, shoe design or even a process for making popsicles**
- What's an untraditional creation that can be patented or protected
- **A Kid Patented the Popsicle** by accident... do you know how?
- **Patent Infringement** means you copied someone's design, secret formula, or creation
- Patents are important for making maximum profit fast and should be done when creating a unique process or invention that solves a problem people are willing to pay for

- Telling your **Krabby Patty formula** to the patent office makes it publicly available, and that is why Coca-Cola made their secret formula **a trade secret instead**

Famous Patents You Should Know About:

- George Washington Carver- peanut butter
- Frank Epperson- Popsicle
- Garrett Morgan – the traffic light
- Marie Van Brittan Brown- the first home security system
- Patricia Era Bath – the blood bank
- George Crum- potato chips
- Madame C.J. Walker - black hair care products
- Gerald A. Lawson- the Fairchild Channel F led to other play at home video game consoles
- Shirley Jackson – technology responsible for Caller ID
- Mark Dean – IBM's first personal computer and color monitor
- Lonnie Johnson- mega water gun (i.e., the super soaker)
- Lisa Gelobter- web animation

Draw What You Learned:

LESSON
08: Education + Money

The Story of Penelope and Roger

Penelope was the most excited kid when it came to applying for school. She talked to her friend Roger about what she wanted to do when she could, and one thing that she knew for sure was that she wanted to do for a living was to design clothes. Now, Roger was quite different, and he was a logical brain kid who really wanted to argue for a living. The best example that Roger had of that was to be a lawyer. Penelope asked Roger a really big question one day and it was, "how will you pay for school?" Roger, who usually had the answer for everything, did not know what to say. In fact, he was floored by the question itself because he didn't have a plan for once in his life, and that scared him. So, they found the guidance counselor at the school, and the best thing that she told them was to apply for something called a scholarship.

They had no idea where to start, and they definitely were not sure if they were even eligible. So, Penelope called her friend Leyoncé who told them about her friend named NeNe. NeNe was watching TV when Penelope called her in complete and total panic. Penelope knew that if she didn't find a way to pay for school that she wouldn't be able to go and design clothes for a living. The first thing that Penelope asked was, "how do I find scholarships to pay for school?" NeNe's advice was to utilize technology in order to be able to reduce the time spent on the Internet looking for scholarships that were sometimes not the best and might not be a good match.

The first site that NeNe recommended was Scholly. This site actually allows an applicant to fill out all of their demographic information and helped match people with the right scholarships for them. The next site that NeNe recommended was a site called FAFSA. This site, unlike other sites, was about trying to find federal student loans and even something called a Federal Pell Grant. Now we all know that paying for school ain't cheap, but if you can find the scholarship especially at undergraduate where you spend at least four years or in graduate school where you spend two to three sometimes five years, then you might actually have a chance at success. Many students are actually crippled with student loan debt later on so you NeNe did not want Penelope and Roger to struggle like she did once upon time with student loans if avoidable.

Roger was next and he had a lot of questions especially because he wanted to go to law, and he wanted to make sure that he was applying to the schools to give him his best chance for success. The last thing that NeNe told them about was the PSAT scholarship given to National Merit Scholarship Award Winners. Penelope and Roger looked completely confused because they thought the PSAT was just a test that teachers made them take for continued testing torture.

NeNe told them that this test was critical for her going to college completely free because. At one point in time, they had something called the **National Achievement Program which allowed for minority kids to have an opportunity to get a full ride scholarship (a.k.a. everything's paid for)**. However, they changed the program dramatically. They **got rid of the program for minority kids to qualify** based on test inequalities which means all students have to study even harder for this test **to beat the testing bell curve.**

The only qualifying score for the PSAT that will determine whether or not you can get this specific honor **occurs in your 10th grade year of high school.** Scoring high on this test can mean a full ride scholarship to any college. Penelope and Roger were only eighth graders, so they had plenty of time to prepare for this test. Roger and Penelope asked the school guidance counselor about whether or not they had a **PSAT tutoring program.** To their luck, they actually did have a program at their school, but most students didn't ask for it.

They quickly enrolled and two years later they both were able to score as **National Merit Semi-Finalists.** They had to **write an essay and turn in letters of recommendation to get the finalist status,** but after that, Roger and Penelope could go anywhere. It was literally **one test score that changed their lives. They were so happy because money was no longer a barrier for them.**

01. What do you think a scholarship is?

02. Why did Roger and Penelope want to go to college?

03. Why did Roger and Penelope get worried?

04. What made both Roger and Penelope the happiest?

What You Will Learn Today:

The lessons throughout this section are for those who have struggled with understanding education after high school and how to finance it. There are so many websites they never show us until high school or even college where you can obtain scholarships. The hardest thing to do is building a plan. If you start early, you can set yourself up for success for certain exams that can lead to **full-ride scholarships.** The lesson goes into how sometimes your school doesn't always inform you of ways to go to college for free outside of the normal student loans recommendation and the occasional scholarship application. We will also cover how sports are not the only way out to get education, but instead strategic planning for your money needs in schools at an earlier age like starting a **college fund.** It is up to you to make a list of scholarship sources you have. Think about asking your **local church, non-profits, the Federal Pell Grant program, and bigger scholarship foundations including companies like banks, law firms, and professional associations.**

Together, we will learn how to create our passport to anywhere we want to go for our education by preparing with more than just sports. We have the ability to use our minds and advance planning to find scholarships earlier and apply often. You can **be SCHOLARSHIP RECIPIENT** right now with an inventive mind, a **disciplined spirit, and A MOTIVATION TO BE DEBT FREE AND HAVE A PAID EDUCATIONAL EXPERIENCE.**

A Note To Keep In Mind:

- **HBCUs are great schools** (contrary to what the ranking says)- the opportunities at Historically Black Colleges and Universities (HBCUs) can truly transform lives because as a kid you might not have seen as many successful minority leaders growing up, but at an HBCU they are everywhere

- **Diversity** at a school also means inclusive ways of teaching of both sides of an issue, but it doesn't mean using stereotypes to define people

- **Letters of Recommendation** are the best letters you can obtain from people who have seen your work ethic and can tell others very well in a written form how amazing you are

Values to Learn:

Although one can have many school choices and scholarships, how will you be remembered?

- Being creative with ways to solve problems can include **using technology to find an automated solution, doing research on the process you do not understand, or using the resources you have available to you**

- What's an untraditional education route can include: **community college, associate's programs, cosmetology school, barber school, massage therapy, plumbing school, and more**

- **A Scholarship Comes with Certain Rules** you must follow to keep it... what if you lose it?

- Work study or jobs at the school you go to can help alleviate the pressure of needing student loans

- While getting an education is important, being a victim of burnout can occur if you try to push through school without stopping. **Think about study abroad opportunities**

Money Hustles for You:

- **Scholly** - costs a small membership fee, but matches you to scholarships for school
- **FAFSA** - you might as well get familiar with this because in case you lose your scholarship, you will need to request student aid
- **Church** - there are funds in the church that you can request for
- **Sororities and Fraternities** - scholarship pageants
- **Business Associations for professionals** - these are usually niche specific, but there are still opportunities for funding
- **National Merit Finalist program via PSAT** - do your research on this test and prepare early. Still a full ride available

Draw What You Learned:

LESSON
09: Struggling + Money

The Story of Mud Jones

Mud Jones dreamed of being rich since he was younger. He had grown up in the inner-city and his mom and dad **barely had two pennies to keep the m afloat when he was younger.** However, Mud was **always able to eat and had a warm bed to sleep in.** For that fact, Mud was always thankful. Mud was exceptionally great at sports and thought he was going to go to the league. In Mud's mind that was the only way out of the neighborhood he grew up in. His dad, Mr. Jones, was sitting at the table one morning reading the newspaper when Mud burst out and said, **"I'm tired of being broke, Dad. I want to be able to buy the things I want too not just the things I need!"**

Mr. Jones looked at his son Mud for what seemed like forever. He folded the newspaper neatly. He placed it softly on the table, cut his eggs in his plate into bite size pieces and used the salt and pepper seasoning to make it taste the way he liked. After five minutes of silence, Mud was preparing for the fate of most kids who yell things out at the table, a whooping. However, Mr. Jones just said," It's okay to be mad. However, if you don't like something son, **it's up to you to change your reality."**

Mud looked at his dad who had given such long speeches in the past, and he looked different. The next question that Mr. Jones asked was, "Mud, what does it mean to be broke to you?" Mud answered quickly, "basically us right now, barely any money to buy most things and you are always living paycheck to paycheck." What Mr. Jones said next lit a fire under Mud for many years to work on being more appreciative of what he had.

Mr. Jones took a long sigh, and said, "Son, it is time I told you how I met your momma. I was a young kid not much older than you and we didn't have much. I had a small job delivering newspapers that barely paid me anything. One day, on my route, I saw the most beautiful girl in the world. She was sitting and waiting on the stoop, and I was wondering why she was up so early. As soon as I got close to her house, she lit up, and me being the full of myself, the kid thought it was because she "liked me." Your momma was waiting on that newspaper because her dad never really let her see it once it got in the house, and she loved finding out what was happening in the world. She told me this once, but I never understood how much she loved it until she was outside that day."

She would only have ten minutes to read it before she had to give it to her dad. So, with the little money I made, I gave her a second newspaper every time I stopped by and took it out of my check from that day on. She was shocked because I told her every day that somehow, I had an extra newspaper for her, but she knew what I did. She told me years later that that one thing I did was so important to her when she considered taking me seriously. That smile on your momma face was the day I knew I was in love. She lit up with her own newspaper to herself, and she collected them for years. I didn't know your mom wanted to be a writer **one day.** All I knew was to make sure she had what she needed. I knew that was in my power, and I knew that **extra newspaper** could make her smile.

By this point, NeNe Trillionaire walked into the room, and there she was reading her own newspaper and circling stories she liked and deals she could find. Mud never knew why they each had their own newspaper every morning. Now, he did. She looked up and smiled because her husband had always managed to pull her out of her newspaper trance with that story. She looked at Rob and said, "if you are telling that story, which means Mud ain't appreciating what he got right now." Rob chuckled, "well you know our little boy is part of that new Jordans every week generation.

Mr. Jones continued, "Anyways, the important lesson I learned was that getting your mom a second newspaper was the most I had, and I used it to make your mom feel as special as she is. She valued that I gave all I had to make her life easier. The way you define the word "broke" may be someone who is struggling paycheck to paycheck, but there are rich people every day who are miserable because they never paid attention to the little things in life that they did have.

We never wanted to raise you with barely any money, but each day, as long as we can make sure you have food, a place to sleep, and a chance to get a good education, and a loving home, then you are the richest kid in the world. The rest of the stuff you want is extra and meaningless if you can't be happy with what you have now." Mud looked up at his dad, and all he could say was "Dad, I'm sorry for my statement earlier, you are right, I'm really going to appreciate what I have now starting with this newspaper." Mud's mom, NeNe, smiled watching him pick up the newspaper and reading the latest headlines and said, "I think you will be just fine after all, kiddo."

01.   What do you think broke means?

02.   Why did Mud get mad that he was "broke"?

03.   What did Rob buy to impress NeNe?

04.   What made both Rob and NeNe the happiest?

I Want To Be a Trillionaire When I Grow Up

What You Will Learn Today:

The lessons throughout this section are for those who have struggled with understanding money's value in our lives and aren't the best managers of the money they do get. There will an introduction of the virtual game **Spent** to see how each student manages money, $1,000 for a month. They will be forced to make financial decisions that affect how much money they have . The lesson goes into what it means to go bankrupt.

Where does all your money go when you spend it and how can you learn to live below your means? Reflect on those questions since many struggle with money because of a lack of education, lack of access, and lack of planning. But this section makes you think **if you only had $100 how would you multiply it and how to set boundaries in saving money.**

A Note To Keep In Mind:

- **Credit Cards** - when people find themselves struggling to make ends meet, they will often find themselves getting into more debt with these, and **the biggest step to note is to always pay these off in full before the payment date in order to get the money benefits a credit card comes with**
- **Emergency fund** - two to three months' salary should be saved in a savings account just in case you fall on hard times or lose your job. Ask your parents if they have an emergency fund
- **Layaway/Financing** - just because you don't have the most money in the world doesn't mean you can't have nice things or pay for the help you need. Ask for a payment plan or financing option

Values to Learn:

Although one can debts we face, how will you be remembered?

- The Value of Thoughtful Actions can be worth more than money
- Using an attitude of gratitude can lead to happiness you never knew was possible
- Being creative with ways to solve problems can include **making sure you use coupons at the store, take advantage of free food at work, or using me hand me down clothes instead of getting the newest things**
- What can struggling with money look like: **not being able to buy all the groceries you need, dodging bill collectors, paying only the light and water bills instead of the cable bill, spending money too fast, buying all the newest things**
- A Famous Rapper you know filed for Bankruptcy... do you know who?
- What happens when you lose all your money?
- You are not always gonna have money, please be nice to people you meet facing that battle
- Take classes to help you manage money, and learn the basics of how to balance a checkbook or set up a bank account
- Don't buy everything, budget and save for things, and learn to live in a budget

Money Hustles for You:

- **Personal Credit** - get a low limit credit card when you begin and pay it off each month
- **SBA** - Small Business Administration has free classes and workshops to teach you how to manage your business funds and learn how to manage money
- **Banks** - every banking institution, money provider, or even investment company has FREE and reliable financial resources, workshops, and classes
- **Loans** - these are things you have to pay back, but you may be able to ask for microloans to fund small startup ventures
- **Business incubators** - these are usually places where the resources are provided to business minded people to get the connections and resources to launch their idea
- **Libraries** - when you fall on hard times and cannot afford books, Wi-Fi, or internet, you can always tap into this resource to get back on your feet

Draw What You Learned:

LESSON
10: Debt + Money

The Story of Stacy's Bad Credit

Stacey **never paid her bills back;** she got a **credit card her senior year of high school** and never looked back. Every time she reached her limit, she just got a new credit card. Throughout college, she always tried to have the latest fashion and used her card instead of paying with her bank card. Halfway through college, her YouTube channel made it big, and she was starting to get some **major brand deals.**

Stacey realized that she needed to **get her money game right,** so she tried to hire a **bookkeeper.** She gave her all the **back-owed credit card bills** and said that she wanted to try to pay these off finally. They told her it would be **$5,000 to balance her books** and try to figure out how to get her on the right path. Stacey was shocked that the price was that high and decided to see if she could fix her money problems on her own. She paid the **minimum on all the cards, but the interest kept rising,** and she felt like she was in a hole she couldn't escape. Stacey was not someone who couldn't be easily defeated, so she called her friend Shante and asked if she knew anyone who was good with understanding money.

Shante told her about NeNe. NeNe had been writing articles for years trying to get people to **learn more about financial literacy and trademarks and business,** but no one would listen. This group of friends kept referring business to her. NeNe was so happy. She was finally able to save money for Mud's college and a family vacation. This time she decided that after she helped Shante that this was something she was skilled at, so she would build a consulting business and charge for her advising.

Shante told NeNe that she had **racked up $15,000 in debt on her five credit cards, and she had no idea nor any strategies she had to pay them down.** NeNe asked Shante, "do you have any money coming in right now?" She said, yes "I get $1,000 for my YouTube videos each month and I work as a tutor at my school and get $500 per month from that job." NeNe asked Shante if she had ever heard of the **20-30-50 budgeting rule?** She hadn't.

NeNe explained, "your bills cost a certain amount per month, so assume from this point on that your check has to be used to pay majority of it. **50% until you pay everything off can go to your bills. That means that with the remaining 30% you save for a rainy day,** and the other 20% you use on your wants or needs. Do this every month for six months, and tell me your progress? While you are doing that, pick a skill that you are good at and figure out how to increase your income or reduce your bills either by more content creation or more hours at your school job or even moving back home."

Stacey tried this for six months, and she took time to really improve her YouTube channel. Stacey even went to the bank to ask for a loan to help, but they denied her because her credit score was so bad. Stacey finally got the amount owed down to $8,000. **She spent the majority of her checks on the bills and moved back in with her folks to save money** on other bills. When she came back to NeNe, she was still stressed, but she could breathe.

The hardest thing for Stacey was learning that all the bad decisions she made back in high school and the first two years of college had really set her back. She had never thought about saving money for the future. She always wanted to be in the in-crowd, but in **doing this savings plan that NeNe showed** her, she felt a sense of relief of doing something on her own. It was extremely hard to come out of that hole, but by the year mark, she had paid all of it back and the interest too, She was **so relieved that she paid NeNe her half of her next paycheck as a thank you for her advice.**

NeNe was floored because she had been giving free advice so long, she had never imagined someone seeing her value. She **used that money to file for her official LLC and she launched the NeNe Trillionaire Consulting Firm.** Stacey was her first loyal customer, and she signed up for monthly calls. Stacey finally broke free from credit cards for large amounts, and she started looking for the credit card benefits instead. Now, she knows how to make her credit card work in her favor and has a nice nest egg for savings.

01.   What do you think a bookkeeper means?

02.   Why did Stacey say no to the bookkeeper?

03.   What did Stacey use to reduce her debt?

04.   Why did Stacey pay NeNe so much for her advice?

What You Will Learn Today:

This lesson focuses on the **20-30-50 budgeting method.** This section is centered on **how important it is to pay off debts.** And although it is better in the long-term this section simplifies good debt which includes credit that one can pay off immediately. The lessons throughout this section are for those who have struggled with understanding the importance of paying off your debt and trying to manage money more wisely, **so you won't get in a financial hole.**

Debt is a huge stressor for many people in today's world, and it can be the main reason people cannot have opportunities to expand or even buy things like an apartment or home. Being a good repayer of your debts actually reaps many rewards, and if you do not know how there are many resources that you can go to get a better handle on your credit and debt issues. The other amazing option is that you **can use credit to benefit you if you think of paying everything off right after you use your credit card.**

A Note To Keep In Mind:

NerdWallet - breaks down credit cards and benefits to using them and finding one to match yours

Experian - please make an account and pay the fee so you can see all three of your credit scores and lock your account in case of any bad guys using your info without your permission

Debt Envelopes - you might not be able to save money well, and maybe to pay back folks, you need to put the money truly out of sight, so consider envelopes for debt instead

Values to Learn:

Although one can debts we face, how will you be remembered?

- The Value of Paying Down Debt slowly can be helpful

- Using an attitude of self-love can lead to avoid spending money to keep up with "trends"

- Being creative with ways to solve problems can include **getting multiple jobs to pay off bills faster, asking for odd jobs like lawn mowing, babysitting, dog walking, and asking the bill company for a payment plan**

- What can debt with money look like: **a credit card bill that you cannot pay off, a bounced check, and over drafted bank account, not being able to pay all your bills, a subscription you can no longer afford, a payment for a car or house that's late, having your car taken away because you didn't pay the bill**

- **Do you know what happens to your credit score if you bank account is negative** spent all his money on new outfits early in his career... **do you know if it increases or lowers?**

- You are not limited if you find yourself in debt, and it's not to be ashamed of

- When you find yourself in debt, don't look for them to be forgiven, look for ways to pay them off slowly because they will keep increasing.

- Telling your folks, you are in debt can be scary and hard, but it is better you change the way you view debt. It shows that you are human, and some of us do not always make the best decisions with money, but it doesn't mean we cannot break free. We can decide today to make rules for ourselves that will help us stay protected –**The big difference between you and becoming wealthy is your lack of discipline.**

Money Hustles for You:

- **Amazon Prime Business Credit Card** - this card can really help those of you who are looking for amazon deals and want to use your credit to pay off your amazon bills

- **Costco Visa Credit Card** - this card comes with no international fees and also gives you money back each month for spending

- **Legacy Credit Union Bank Cards** - some of these accounts can come with a reward for spending a certain number of times per month

- **Credit Repair** - there are people who specialize in being able to help you fix their credit score, but please proceed carefully

- **Credit Score** - this score determines whether or not you will be able to be trusted to pay your bills or whether you are too risky for people who rely on you to be dependable

- **Paying the Minimum** - doing this is a good thing to do until you can get back on your feet, but do not make this a habit

Draw What You Learned:

LESSON
11 : Investing + Money

The Story of Shawna's First Investment

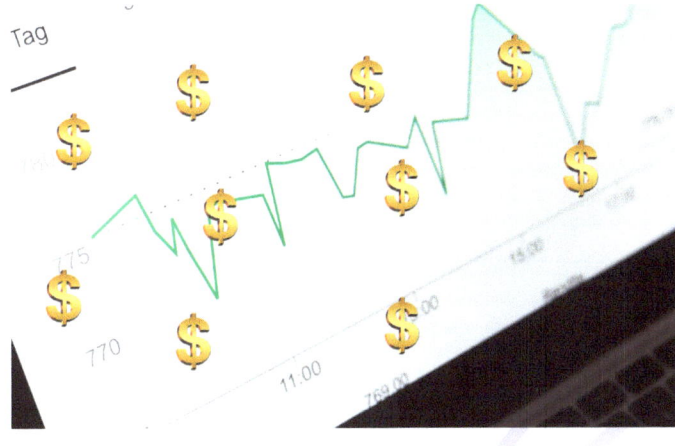

Shawna wanted to grow her money without spending it. She read somewhere that you could buy certain parts of a business and be able to be paid if their business does well. Shawna only had $1,000 to invest and she had been on Instagram searching for education content on it. She kept running into **Forex, Cryptocurrency, and Trading** gurus who asked her for some money that they would then invest for her. She read about something called a **blessing loom** where you recruit other people in a circle and give money to those who recruit more, but she was overwhelmed with what she was finding online.

She downloaded some apps to make some small purchases that were called **fractional investments** like buying a piece of one piece of the company. If one piece of the **business (a share)** costs $30, then she paid $5 for the same piece so she owned 1/6 of the piece. However, she wasn't seeing any real returns. So, she went to find her friend Kira because she remembers that she had a financial literacy consultant friend that told her some tips that really helped her grow her dance business.

Kira quickly called her contact NeNe who went from writing a column on financial literacy to a consulting business. Kira asked NeNe if she could book a paid call with her, Shawna, and herself because she wanted to repay her friend that had supported her dancing all these years. Kira told Shawna that she would talk with her more at the meeting because she was excited to learn too.

NeNe called them both using Google Meet, and when she finished getting some upfront questions answered, she told them about **investments at different levels.** She said there were things called **safe investments** like a money market account available via **Marcus by Goldman Sachs** that only required $1 being placed in an account that earns interest each year. She told them about less risky stocks like mutual funds or groups of stocks that gives them a small piece of multiple high performing companies. She finally told them about volatile investments which could be day trading or stocks that go up and down quickly. NeNe recommended that they both consider taking **free classes through their local bank.**

Neither Shawna nor Kira knew that banks teach this kind of information and that was something that inspired them both. They asked where they could go to find more information like this. NeNe replied, I would look into companies like Stockpile, which is a good app for purchasing fractional stocks. All of these companies put out free resources on their websites that can teach you this. She also mentioned companies like AmeriTrade, and their online resources. Lastly, she mentioned getting a money wealth adviser. One company she remembered her family used was TIAA.

Shawna and Kira downloaded Stockpile and bought stock in companies they loved like Starbucks, **Ferrari, and Disney.** They also looked at stock advice from financial social media influencers who have done well with their money. They went to show their parents, and even their parents hadn't heard of this app. The parents in the community were having a block party and Kira and Shawna's parents started showing the other parents the free classes offered at their local banks. They all decided to go to one workshop together. After the workshop, the parents realized that this should be taught to their kids, and they asked each other how they could request this. One of the parents knew **a city council member and asked if they could present a proposal at the next meeting.** They said yes.

The parents called NeNe and asked if she would be able to come to the meeting and help them prepare a program proposal. NeNe decided to try her best to **write a proposal for the parents to advocate for funding for this project.** The parents asked questions about how NeNe knew all this stuff. She explained how she had **struggled with money for years** with Mud's dad and instead of just dealing with it, she decided to ask questions. **After that, she decided to help more people learn this.** The parents were blown away that they had someone so enthusiastic about their kids learning. One day, they were talking and realized that she had helped each of their kids with a money problem all these years for free.

01. What do you think an investment means?

02. What did Shawna and Kira teach their parents?

03. What did the parents decided to change?

04. Why did they call NeNe?

What You Will Learn Today:

This lesson focuses on the investment options that kids are not often told about until later. This section is centered on the many ways to invest including stocks, NFTs, Trading, and more. This section relates to if one can invest in a business and make money from it. Investing is putting up something of value to have the opportunity to make more money. Contemplate where would you invest?

A few good investments are health insurance, car insurance, and life insurance. This section delves deeper into planning for the future and your goals. This section is about what lifestyle you would want to live. It is important to think about what you want to be when you grow up and how you would like to earn income with your gifts and talents and the role model in your life.

This section also teaches us how younger generations can teach their parents and change a community with equal access to information. When the parents and younger generations unite at an early age, they can change the way future kids are taught.

A Note To Keep In Mind:

- **Investopedia** - a dictionary online that helps people understand investment terms and expand their knowledge in money management

- **Roth IRA vs. Traditional IRA** - Roth IRA is taxed now and you will not pay taxes on it later, Traditional IRA is not taxed now, but will be taxed later (both are retirement accounts you can setup now)

- **Pitch Decks** - these are used to tell someone with money about how your business idea is so unique and worth investing in to help you make more of your product faster or increase you impact with their skills in a way that makes you both money

- **Business Proposal** - this is often used in grant applications or requests for funding for big business ventures that requires funding for specific purpose in alignment with a community need

- **ROI** - this means return on investment and is often used to describe when something you paid for gives you back more than what you paid for it

Values to Learn:

Although one can have investment options, how will you be remembered?

- The Value of Investing early in life can be helpful

- Using a community of support and collaboration can lead to change for the better that you never knew was possible

- Being creative with ways to solve problems can include investing in stocks, taking some trader courses, listening to the investment podcasts, joining investment groups that explain key terms without getting salesy

- **Who are can investors who support Black owned businesses: The Fearless Fund (launched by Keisha Knight Pulliam and Ariana Simone), Rough Draft Ventures (supports student-led startups funded by students), Black Angel Tech Fund (invested in OmniSpeech), Ruben Harris (Career Karma -mentorship in careers and coding bootcamps), Hustle Fund (invests to reduce inequalities)**

- **A Famous Model Investor you know that only invests based on her values... do you know who?**
- What happens when you invest in your friend's business?
- You are not always unless a ton of money to invest, but don't forget you are your best investment
- Invest in things you care about

Money Hustles for You:

- **Ameritrade -** here you can open your own brokerage (which is another word for an account that lets you own stocks and more) and purchase on the open market
- **Money Watch Stock Market Simulator -** virtual game with tons of ads that you can play for free that lets you experience the stock market by not investing much Stockpile - you can buy a piece of stock for $1 and work your way towards owning a full share but still get some opportunity to make money
- **Robinhood -** is a great place to buy fractional, stock but be careful, it is ridiculously hard to closes your account later
- **Marcus -** by Goldman Sachs is a money market savings account and more and it allows you to invest a minimum of $1 towards savings and has a much higher interest rate so you can earn money by just leaving it there
- **529 Plan -** is a tax beneficial account you can create to set aside money for school as a scholarship
- **Kiva Loans -** you can make money by investing startup funds into other businesses

Draw What You Learned:

LESSON
12: Planning + Money

The Story of Penelope the Event Planner

Penelope was the assistant to someone who sat on the city council, and she would write up pitch ideas all the time for something amazing that could help the city, but she never felt confident enough to pitch it. Penelope was best friend's with Leyonce's mom and found herself in the middle of a huge planning meeting with NeNe and all the parents to have influence in the schools and she remembered that her Councilman she worked for was asking the office to pitch ideas on financial literacy. She was really excited to get started on a pitch, but she had no idea what people did not understand about money, and she had no one to teach it in the schools, and so she scrapped her idea because she didn't want to plan her first big project poorly.

However, whether it be fate or a miracle from her fairy godmother, she knew that she could find her confidence to pitch her ideas. NeNe asked the group, "What problem are we trying to solve?" Penelope said, "we are solving the problem of students and families not having equal access to financial literacy lessons regarding budgeting, saving or managing money in schools, organizations, and beyond.

NeNe smiled and exclaimed, "That's right Penelope!" Leyonce's mom was just so excited to see her friend finally share her voice that had been quiet for so long. The rest of the parents started trying to come u[with the hook to make the City Council care, and they decided to start with the Values and Money lesson that NeNe taught Leyoncé and Shante about how they could go down to the local thrift store or go on eBay to find the same items for less money but more importantly how things like friendship were built on understanding your values and what you believe in when it comes to spending money and that's the mark of a truly fulfilled life.

The next lesson they had was about Social Media and Money where NeNe taught Kira how to build her own dance community using her social media accounts while also stressing the importance to use social media for more than just a time waster, but a connection creator. Then, finally teaching their Leyoncé how to demand a salary for herself that she wanted with her lesson in Jobs and Money.

There were so many other lessons NeNe taught them from Business, to Trademarks, to Copyrights, to Patents, to Education, to Struggling, to Debt, to Investing and finally to Planning. However, NeNe made sure to tell them that making money wasn't as important as developing good values, good connections, and good goals that they could be proud of when they shared their story.

Each kid's story was valuable and NeNe and the parents could think of no better way to say this than to tell each of their stories one by one in a book. Each kid's story was captured, and the parents happily let NeNe, the group journalist retell the stories. Penelope was put in charge of the event planning before the pitch.

Penelope interviewed Leyoncé who was saving money and investing in her friend's business. She spoke to Kira was launching dance communities and NeNe's son Mud who finally knew how to appreciate the little things. She even talked to Sketch and Pike who NeNe got to talk to again , and the craziest part of these small lessons is that each of these keys helped the kids go back and impact their parents.

Every kid went back and asked their parents to start custodial bank accounts and money market accounts to start planning for the future. NeNe with her knowledge and background in business and law had taken her knowledge and helped a whole village raise financially savvy kids. They had businesses and thought of patents and the parents saw the success stories. They saw their kids changing, asking   hard questions even they didn't ask growing up.

NeNe with her consulting business had opened so many doors in her own community, but the parents believed that more students needed this support. Kira's mom had a Program Director role at a local HBCU, and Penelope asked if they could hold a book club for new authors. Kira's mom pitched it to her team, and they approved and purchased 100 copies for each of their students to read. This is where NeNe had her first official reading of the book, and it was something amazing. Leyoncé took pictures and did a book review for the book and agreed to support NeNe's consulting business as a brand ambassador.

The parents found a grant that the city was offering and incorporated NeNe as the instructor. Penelope was finally taking this plan to the next level. She outlined a budget that broke down how much time it would take to complete a solid program, pay the instructor/speaker NeNe, and make the program impactful for the students for years to come. She found sponsors for this and put together a business plan with NeNe that outlined the 1 Year, 3 Year, 5 Year and 10 Year plans for growth. They held interest meetings with other parents and hosted a book club to show the lessons NeNe would teach. The parents in ten districts were ready to sign up.

The kids there had started implementing the lessons, and finally Penelope was ready to pitch at the next city council meeting. She gave her boss a heads up before, and Penelope and NeNe stood should backed by 100 parents and kids ready to get the program started. After hearing the pitch, Penelope's boss stood up and said...

01. What do you think happened after the pitch?

02. What did Penelope do to help?

03. What did NeNe teach the kids?

04. How did they plan for the future?

What You Will Learn Today:

This lesson focuses on the idea behind planning ahead for success. Many of those who want to achieve anything memorable must first learn that discipline, consistency, and proper timing is the most critical factor to being able to win. We also learn that we don't have to know if the ending will result in a "happily ever after" result because fairy tales are not the only possible gain. The beauty of working together and learning teamwork can be so much more powerful, and even if an idea doesn't get funding, there was a ton of supporters who have more influence than others.

An outline for your papers, for your business, for your money spending habits and more can make a huge difference in your life because when you can visualize the steps you need, **you can see the path you need to take.** When you first learned how to drive, you learned the rules of the road. Much like planning your driver license, once you learn the **lingo,** then the only way to evaluate the knowledge is to apply it to real-life scenarios. Sometimes things will work, and sometimes they won't. **The beauty is trying anyway.**

A Note To Keep In Mind:

- **Planners** - don't just let this collect dust or write things in it for a month that you never do. You can buy planner sheets at Hobby Lobby and make your own that fit the way your mind works
- **To-Do Lists** - some people are more detail oriented with the steps to achieve a goal, and do better breaking each step into smaller steps
- **Mind Mapping** - some people work better by writing out there plans in undefined spaces, try buying graph paper or a art sketch book and plan it by drawing things in the abstract and piecing together later
- **Brain Dump** - getting ideas onto paper is the hardest step, try just writing everything that comes to mind about a particular topic and picking the best idea that you write
- **Outlines** - when you make an outline before doing something, it will save you time later and make ideas flow together more naturally

Planning For the Future Money Technique to Outlines

- **(I)ssue:** Define the Problem that you are facing
- **(R)ule:** Figure out the rules and your own core values of how to operate in that money hustle
- **(A)pplication:** Find ways to apply solutions to the problem that does not break your own core values
- **(C)onclusion:** Find the lesson in the struggle even if you cannot solve the problem

Values to Learn:

Although one can have many plans, how will you be remembered?

- The Value of planning with others can be helpful

- Using your passion and creativity can lead to bonds that you never knew were possible

- Being creative with ways to solve problems can include using your resources, connections, talents, and skills in a way to achieve your vision for yourself

- Planning tools you'll love: **Google Keep, Notes, Google Calendar, Miro on Google Meet, Whiteboards, Excel Spreadsheets, Trello, Click Up, Hootsuite**

- In law school, they taught us IRAC, do you know what that stands for?

- What happens when you plan for things instead of just reacting?

- You are not always gonna have a plan, but when you can try something using a method that works, values that you believe in, and your own unique brand

- Don't be afraid to share your ideas or think they are not good enough. You are worth listening to.

Money Hustles for You:

- **Planning for the Life You Want** - this means that you figure out how much money you want to make and what your core rules will be in making it

- **Planning for Retirement** - this doesn't have to happen when you are in your 60s, you can think about how you could do this earlier, ask about 401Ks, Retirement Accounts, and company long-term benefits

- **Planning for School** - think about the cost of living. Make a spreadsheet of all the schools based on 4 factors and visit:

- **4 Factors Test:**

  - Distance
  - Cost
  - Program YOU want
  - Student support
  - There should be a fifth factor based on the visit or communication style between the school and you.

- **Planning for Adult-Life** - the best advice I can give you is to find something you love, and you'll never have to work again

- **Planning for Love** - love yourself first, build your confidence often, then when you're 30 you can consider it, lol JK but seriously

Draw What You Learned:

NeNe Says Do This

10 TIPS THAT WILL SAVE YOUR BUSINESS MONEY

Do you want to start a new business but lack the funds, LISTEN, LISTEN, LISTEN LINDA. YOU DON'T NEED ALLLL THAT. Your first priority your first 2-5 years of business is to KEEP OVERHEAD LOW. I'm only telling you WHAT I KNOW!

1. GOOGLE IS FREE: business name email, Google Drive, Google my Business (I had been using neenaspeeresq@gmail.com for almost three years now before I got a new one. Trust me in time you will get a business email)

2. A P.O. Box IS AFFORDABLE: stop thinking you need to buy an office! That's overhead costs you don't need and can cripple your business in its beginning years if you don't bring in the clientele to make ends meet EVERY MONTH

3. WORDPRESS is FREE: you can make your blog posts on there and not upgrade the domain. (I was using https://takingalunchwithattorneyspeer.wordpress.com/ when I first started, and it still looks beautiful!)

4. BUSINESS PHONE NUMBERS ARE FREE: Google Voice is an app you can download for free; it connects to a laptop and landline and your real cell phone and costs $0 and uploads your call logs and texts into a cloud (my Google voice number has been 205.490.8068 since I launched my law firm in April 2018)

5. SCHEDULING APPS like Calendly, which is Black owned, have adjusted with the times and added Zoom integrations and calendar integrations so everything you need is in one location. DO NOT use the paid version until you can afford it. Put your payment link in the event description or maybe as one of the booking questions if it lets you. I still use Calendly to this day

6. If you need a SAVINGS and Business Checking Account, you can use Marcus by Goldman Sachs to create a high yield online savings account and all you need is $1. This allows you to avoid bank fees for having below $500 in the account like most banks charge. You can easily transfer money to your checking from Marcus when you need it.

7. Streamyard is a FREE streaming app that allows you to STREAM LIVE TO YOUR SOCIAL MEDIA PAGES without charging you for the PRO ACCOUNT like ZOOM and you can have up to 5 guests on the free version. However, for new users, you get a trial with all the pro features so you can have 10 guests, logo customization, and unlimited broadcasts

8. If you can get a website built! You can get a custom domain and web hosting on the LOW. There is a business special on IONOS for $1 first month/$8 every month following with unlimited website/storage and 1-year free domain

9. DON'T BUY A CRM, use the basics like an external hard drive, computer hard drive, and cloud drive (Google is free), and figure out a technology filing system and a paper filing system FIRST. Your software is only helpful if you know how you need it organized to be more efficient. Also, CRMs have glitches all the time. I had to stop using Clio for my appointments and my Payments. I went back to my original apps and programs. Calendly and Law Pay. The worst thing you can do for your new business is to become so reliant on your CRM that you have no way to pivot if the system crashes or glitches

10. Lastly. I have FREE COPY of My Amazon Best-Seller Dear Future CEO ®ANI Checklist to send y'all because I really want to see you FORM and PROTECT these businesses, just email bookneeaspeer@gmail.com the word "MONEY HUSTLES"

HOW TO CREATE YOUR GIPHY CHANNEL AND APPLY FOR GIFS

Have A Domain Name

The first thing you need to have is your domain name. This will enable you to apply and create a brand new channel. You can buy a domain name at $ 8 per month

- Creating A New GIPHY Channel
- Type GIPHY on Google
- From your screen, press the join button
- Input your name and username
- Complete the process and create your profile
- Uploading Your Files
- Browse your files that you would like to use.
- Upload the file and That will link your domain to your website page if you include it in the field that says source on EVERY GIF.
- Pick a favorite tag and add your caption

So that's how to create your GIF. Once you upload your files, it will show on the GIF dashboard. That's what allows you to get your traction out there quickly. It also allows you to see the results at the right time.

You have to diversify with your GIFs because you can't just stay in one place all the time. The best way to use your GIFs when you are trending is to source and drive your website links. Then after 5 gifs have been posted, you can create a BRAND CHANNEL. This means you will be searchable on GIF keyboards that are linked pretty much everywhere. However, use your tags wisely so you can distinguish your GIF from all the other ones. Here's a snapshot of my GIF performance since 2020.

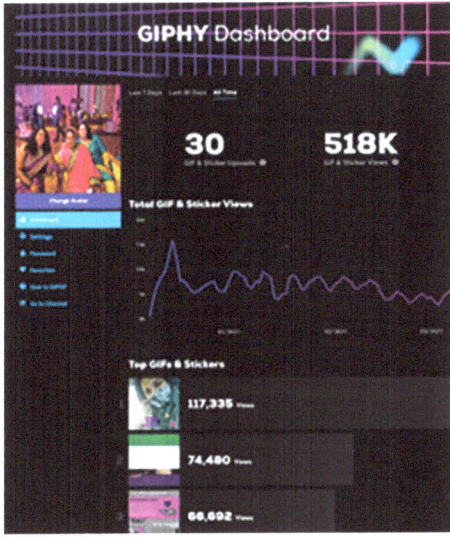

Now, it's your turn. Need help with creating 5 GIFs, email us today for some tips!

Disclaimer: This is for informational use only. Not legal advice. An attorney-client relationship is not formed by viewing and receiving information attached. "No representation is made that the quality of the legal services to be performed is greater than the quality of legal services performed by other lawyers."

5 REASONS WHY YOU NEED AN LLC FOR YOUR NEW BUSINESS

Limited Liability Corporations (or LLCs) are especially important when it comes to protecting your business in your beginning stages. They help you save money tax-wise and have fewer restrictions than you may think.

This pandemic has brought on so much unrest, and you would think that it would have a similar effect on businesses, but it actually has led to more people considering for the first time forming their own businesses. How do I know this? I have put out free content on LLC ownership, trademarks, copyrights, and contracts on my personal social media pages, and I have noticed one major theme: people really want to know 1) how to protect their businesses or 2) how to start up a business No matter what type of business you choose to form, it is important to take precautions to start up a business that works for your needs.

I like a 5-Step Process when I explain concepts to people, so here are my fast five reasons why you need an LLC.

1. You Can Protect Yourself

When you start a business, you probably never knew that your personal assets were on the line before. Most business owners start a sole proprietorship that has the least structure which is good in theory but bad news when you run into a problem. I know we all expect to never have any issues with customers, right? Wrong. We all will eventually face an obstacle in the road, and we do not want to be sued. If you are sued, without an LLC or Corporation, you face some pretty steep liabilities. They can attach the damages to any personal asset you own. Yes, that includes your house, your car, your 401 K, and your personal bank accounts. That sounds kind of scary, right? Yes. The good news is that you will be a strategic and clever business owner, so you will already have that LLC formed. That way your assets are safe, and you can focus on growing and protecting your business. Yes, you may want an LLC, but just know that an LLC can easily become a Corporation later on, but that's another blog.

2. You Can Have Less Structure

Have you wondered why people LOVE LLCs? It is because, unlike corporations, you do not have to observe the normal formalities. Once you have formed your LLC, if you develop an operating agreement (which is a rule book for the way you want the company to run and who owns it) you will not be subject to default rules in your state for compliance. Also, you do not have to run meetings or keep meeting minutes like you would a corporation. (P.S. corporations are what you would create if you wanted to form a non-profit organization. Therefore, my charitable business-minded folks, keep that in mind when you are considering what to form.) Your LLC can also have a charitable proceeds component where you donate a portion of the profits to your charity of choice later on. With non-profits, there are all sorts of restrictions on your money and the kind of money and influence you can take on. There are also restrictions on regular meetings, minutes, and the number of people you need to form one. In Alabama, you need 3 people to form a non-profit, but not for an LLC. You can form an LLC with just you and not have to hold meetings nor create minutes. Isn't that easy?

3. You Can Run It How You Want

Another benefit of the LLC is that if you want to add more leaders later on you can just do so. Of course, you might want to update your operating agreement and re-file to reflect that change, but you do not have to seek majority board approval to make decisions. Alternatively, with a corporation, every decision you make that will adversely or positively affect the company or its shareholders must be voted on by the group. This a great thing when everybody agrees completely, but when you start selling shares, major shareholders gain the right to weigh in and tie your hands from future decisions if they choose to. That is not how an LLC functions, and that should bring you some major relief!

4. You Can See Tax Benefits

Did you know that you are double taxed without an LLC? Corporations, everybody's favorite thing because of the stocks you can sell, are taxed twice. Once on the dividends and once on the income, and people just have no idea. The value of an LLC is that, unlike a sole proprietorship where the business is not taxed separately from the owner, an LLC is not taxed at the entity level which means that the income and losses pass through to the members' (owners') individual tax returns. However, always consult a tax attorney to be certain of all your tax concerns.

5. You Can Modify How You Are Taxed to an S-Corp Later

A lot of people toss around business terms and always mention the term to form an S-Corporation. Just so you know, there is no such thing as an s-corporation as a business entity. However, you can elect to have your LLC and even your Corporation taxed as an S-Corporation. That will come in handy when you are making the big money later on and you can get taxed a bit less if you can designate "a reasonable salary" deduction that you pay yourself consistently. However, a CPA knows best, so make sure before you elect for S-Corp, you reach out to a tax professional.

As always there are tons of online sites to file your LLC, but if you are uncertain or need your questions answered on where to start, instead of using an online application seek out the advice of a legal professional before deciding how to form your LLC or other business structures.

Now, it's your turn. Need help with creating your own business, email us today for some tips!

Disclaimer: This is for informational use only. Not legal advice. An attorney-client relationship is not formed by viewing and receiving information attached. "No representation is made that the quality of the legal services to be performed is greater than the quality of legal services performed by other lawyers."

Virtual Games List

- **Play Spent** - virtual game at playspent.org that gives you a preview of adult life with managing $1000 for 30 days with bills and other responsibilities

- **The Bean Game** - each student is given 20 beans and told that the categories In the game represent everyday needs. Once they have budgeted their bean allowance, then the list of scenarios begins

- **The Estimation Game** - students have to guess in real time the closest price for the items on the board

- **Dollar and a Dream Activity** - this tests the students potential for success with managing a small amount of money and producing a big idea

- **What in the Harriet Tubman, $20 Bill Talk?** – this is a candid conversation about who appears on the money we use and letter writing activity to state why we think Harriet Tubman should be on the $20 bill already

- **The Job Game** - Choose 10 Professions and print the name on one sheet of paper and they have to search for their average salary, 3 examples of people they know in that profession, and the top paid professional in that field

- **Popsicle Logos** - tell the kids about the popsicle patent and tell them to draw their own unique logo on a popsicle stick

- **Make Your Own Money** - this activity allows kids the creativity of making unique money examples as we assign the value of each coin and dollar

- **Mind storming** – make your 20 different skills you can get paid for list

- **Write a Letter to the Older You** – tell yourself in the letter that you believe in yourself.

- **Find the ®/©** - look in the room for a product with a circle R on it

For even more fun and exciting financial literacy games, please ask us more about **how to book Neena at bookneenaspeer@gmail.com**

MEET THE AUTHOR

Neena Speer, Financial Literacy Consultant

ABOUT THE VISION

I equip Title 1 students with the tools to become financially savvy using mathematical principles and problem solving through budgeting, saving, and managing money.

Neena tells her story about how she was born to thrive, not survive, when she nearly lost her life at 6 years of age due to chickenpox encephalitis and how her life has been both amazing in a loving home but riddled with obstacles she never imagined. By the age of eight, Neena produced her first business training manual to pitch to a local non-profit. She worked on it and tried to get it implemented before she graduated high school, but no one would listen to her BIG IDEAS. She kept on creating programming and acting as the proxy leader for many organizations throughout her career, but people would not let her lead. So, she did what any financial genius would do next, "created her own business," but that happened after she did what others wouldn't. Learn the game.

Neena did the busy work, learned the inventory process, and went behind the scenes of many organizations and figured out how to make their systems more efficient. When she went to Howard University, she launched her very own MATH TUTORING business, after many unpaid invoices and IOU's, she finally started tutoring athletes in Math and French formally with Howard Athletics, and that's when teaching math in a fun and unique began and applying her knowledge of financial literacy became something powerful.

In the first year, she learned that hustling ain't all it's cracked up to be if you don't understand the business behind it. After growing with a life-long YMCA relationship as a baby in the nursery, to after-school, to volunteering, to counselor in training, to nursery worker, to nine years as summer camp counselor.

She not only loves kids, but she worked at a non-profit long enough to learn everything she needed to start her own because her bosses had her create counselor schedules, camper schedules, do inventory, and yes even paint some picnic benches without a single complaint from her. Neena uses what she learned to empower kids to learn more about the amazing power of math and problem solving to understand money, business, leadership and making millions.

PROJECT PROPOSAL

KEYNOTE PRESENTATION

One hour presentation to equip students with the tools they need to navigate through financial roadblocks understand the values of money, and strategically being able to balance money, motivations and overcoming failure.

TRILLIONAIRES PROGRAM

This program is designed to help students with values, social media, jobs, inventions/business, trademarks, copyrights, patents, life after school, struggles with debt or money, investing, career readiness, , and managing internal and external conflict to increase confidence, self-esteem, and effective decision-making. *This is done by 1 assembly and 2 breakout sessions with student leadership and students who struggle academically.*

ATHLETIC DEVELOPMENT:

One hour presentation to equip athletes with the tools they need to manage their emotions, create a winning culture, and balance life, sports, and academics.

PROFESSIONAL DEVELOPMENT: (WELCOME TO THE JUNGLE)

W2J: Teaches communication principles that create high-performing teams. The program runs on passion and consistency, and links productivity to business strategy. W2J helps businesses understand the psychology of why people are productive (or not) and how to leverage that information to transform performance and decrease burn out!

NEENASPEER.COM

Are you ready to make money to change the path for your family ?

www.ingramcontent.com/pod-product-compliance
Lightning Source LLC
Chambersburg PA
CBHW050746110526
44590CB00003B/93